# HUMAN HARMONY

KARISHMA D S

ISBN 978-1-68586-533-7

To caffeine, sugar, and the universal solvent.

To all those who spent their valuable money and will be spending their time on my first book.

And lastly to those who made my life existential and meaningful.!

# Contents


*Introduction*                                      *vii*

   1. Decoding E-m-o-t-i-o-n                    1

   2. The Discovery                             7

   3. Those Feels                               9

   4. Journey Of Emo-volution                   15

   5. Emotional Ideologies                      18

   6. Wear That Mask                            25

   7. Emotional Drive                           31

   8. The Roller Coaster Ride                   35

   9. Soudness Of Mind                          40

End Note                                             47

References                                           51

# INTRODUCTION

Human life is disorganized. There is no specific pattern to one's choices or lifestyle. Everyone has their way of dealing with the journey. The systematic planning from birth to death does not exist. There are too many hot and cold days that need survival. And humans do survive every second of wrath as well as glee. There is some harmony that acts as a helping hand. And that harmony is *'emotions'*.

Writing on emotion has been a very emotional journey. I discovered my emotions only after becoming a mother. I was blown away at how a little human being can help you discover your survival skills, patience level and bring out all hidden emotions. Maybe it is all same with everyone. The lemon that life throws on you depend on what you try to make out of it; squeeze them in someone's eye, or make lemonade! That's how emotions are. They are all reactions.

Not everyone reacts to the same situation in the same manner. For a topper getting 90 out of 100 might be the end of the world, and the same marks for an average student might be an Oscar-winning moment. Emotions vary from person to person, gender to gender, culture to culture, place to place.

So while discovering my emotional journey, I had a chance to figure out the literal emotional world. This world of emotion is just as vast as the universe and my exploration lies in mere percentage.

Chapter one is all about the word emotion, what are its types and variations, etc. Next is chapter two, telling you all about how its existence came, when was the term discovered, and how it got its name?

Why do humans feel so much and do animals also feel the pain is described in the third chapter. Read all about Darwin and his research on emotion in chapter four (Yes, emotion is linked to evolution). Chapter five tells about different theories involving emotions (they are not too tacky, read them you won't get bored!).

The face says all, does it? Find this out in Chapter six. Chapter seven will help you deal with your emotion (I hope you find it motivational). This is followed by the highs and lows that occur due to emotions in Chapter eight.

And the last chapter deals with the common problem everyone faces, mental breakdown. Don't forget to read the endnote.

Have an emotional reading!

# I
# Decoding E-M-O-T-I-O-N

Newton's law: to every action, there is an equal and opposite reaction. That last word is your emotion. The biological response to situations happening around us which is either negative or positive. Just like a group of people in a crowd, a group of feelings is emotion. A typical definition can be found on Wikipedia but here is what I figured out.

*"Emotion is brain's reaction towards any situation accompanied by physical changes."*

Not every psychologist might agree with my made-up definition since the meaning of emotion turns out to be a complex one. There have been numerous researches on how emotion works which will be discussed further. For now, let's dig into emotions.

Robert Plutchik's wheel of emotion (refer to color image)

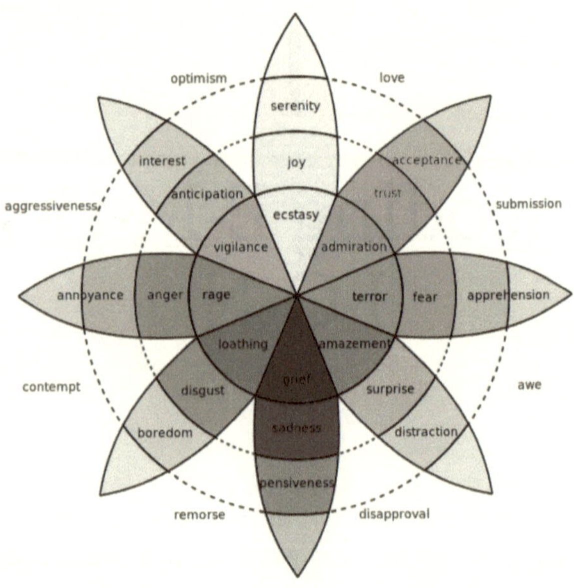


Robert Plutchik's wheel of emotions (refer to color image)

Each one of us has experienced the emotions written on the wheel above. This wheel was constructed by psychologist Robert Plutchik in 1980. This wheel has eight basic emotions organized according to the physiological response, and eight derivative emotions with each composed of two basic ones. He enlisted these emotions just like colors are distributed in a color palette. Like colors, primary emotions can be expressed at different intensities and can mix to form different emotions. Consider emotion as a big ice cream cone that opens to different petals. Each petal has different emotion.

This is how Plutchik's wheel works!

The eight big circles are eight basic emotions: joy, trust, fear, surprise, sadness, disgust, anger, and anticipation. These are called primary emotions. Each primary emotion has an "opposite' emotion. For example, joy and sadness. Two primary emotions can be combined to form a third emotion, also known as the derivative emotion. For example, joy and trust make love.

The rest of the emotions, lying opposite to the basic ones shows how emotion intensifies. For example, emotions intensify as they move from the outside to the center of the wheel, which is also indicated by the color: the darker the shade, the more intense the emotion.

The list of emotions is endless (they are around 34,000). It can be expressed in many ways as depicted in the wheel.

There are three parts to an emotion.

1. Subjective Component: This involves an individual's feelings or his experience in that particular situation. In simple words, identification of emotion.

2. Physiological Component: Once the emotion is identified, the body acts. The chemical reaction happening after any situation is followed, like pulling your hand away from heat.

3. Expressive Component: Communicative function of how a person expresses his experience (facial expressions, hand gestures, body movements, etc.). This differs on the inter-individual level, as well as that of the individual.

Plutchik's wheel of emotion also gives a guide on how emotions are nothing but a survival kit. Activation of emotion is equivalent to survival happening on a subconscious level. Check out the following image.

| Protection | Withdrawal, retreat<br>(activated by fear and terror) |
| --- | --- |
| Destruction | Elimination of barrier to the satisfaction of needs<br>(activated by anger and rage) |
| Incorporation | Ingesting nourishment<br>(activated by acceptance) |
| Rejection | Riddance response to harmful material<br>(activated by disgust) |
| Reproduction | Approach, contract, genetic exchanges<br>(activated by joy and pleasure) |
| Reintegration | Reaction to loss of nutrient product<br>(activated by sadness and grief) |

## Emotion and responses

Let's time travel to the stone age. You see this ferocious creature who is about to attack you. You try to stay calm and save yourself. Your fear makes you protect yourself. That's the relationship between emotions and survival.

> "*Fear is an emotion, indispensable for survival.*
> *-Hanah Arendt*"

The Swiss also have developed another wheel of emotion. The *Geneva Emotion Wheel*! This is a scientific method to measure emotional reactions to objects, events, and situations developed after lots of trial and error. Unlike, Plutchik's wheel, GEW does not have any primary emotion and the intensities of emotions are reversed.

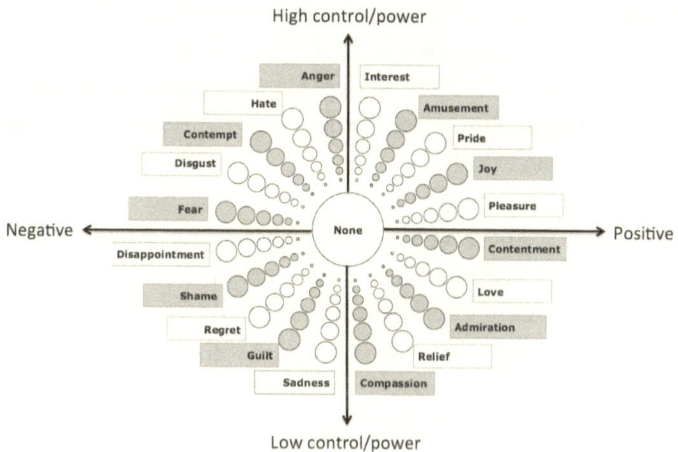


## Geneva Emotion Wheel

According to GEW, 20 emotions are evaluated according to two parameters. These parameters are valence, which describes the situation and other is power/control depicting an individual's capacity to react to that situation. There are many situations when you don't feel like reacting to, GEW has named this as no emotion / other emotion. It also includes two emotion shame and pride that is not found in Plutchik's wheel.

This is how the GEW tool works. You are given a situation or event and response sheet which a GEW image. First, identify approximately what the event that produced the emotion meant to you and choose the emotion family that seems to best correspond to the kind of feeling you experienced when this happened, even though the words on the sheet may not capture all facets of your experience. Then determine with which intensity you experienced the respective emotion and check one of the circles in the "spike" corresponding to this emotion family -- the bigger the circle and the closer it is to the rim of the wheel, the stronger your emotional experience would have been. Different intensities often correspond to different members of an emotion family.

Thus, irritation can be considered a less intense emotion belonging to the Anger family and anxiety a less intense emotion belonging to the Fear family. For less intense emotions, please check one of the smaller circles in the spike. If the emotion was very intense, please check the largest circle of the spike.

This is really interesting, you can try it out!

Though both wheels have a different perspective, both are a good starting point for detecting emotions.

> *"Your emotions make you human. Even the unpleasant ones have a purpose. Don't lock them away. If you ignore them, they just get louder and angrier."*
>
> **—Sabaa Tahir, A Torch Against the Night"**

# II
# The Discovery

Let's start with an emotional history.

"Long long back ago, humans believed that the human mind was controlled by the Almighty. And a devil named emotion lived inside it that could only be controlled using divine powers. A few years later, somewhere in the 19$^{th}$ century, Charles Darwin made an entry who replaced his theories for supernatural powers.

**Psychology was born and the myth was turned into reality.**

This reality was short-lived as the science of emotion fell into the field of human behavior and was not sciency enough for researchers to study. Emotion fell into the world of darkness for at least 50 years. In the 1950s, various disciplines like psychology, linguistics, computer science, anthropology, neuroscience, and philosophy were grouped into a class of science called cognitive science. This cognitive revolution helped emotions to *be rediscovered and we know them now as our survival kit.*

*Thus, we all lived happily, sadly, angrily, etc ever after.* "

This story has a different version in different psychology books. The word emotion though dates back to 1579, adapted from the French word *émouvoir*, meaning to stir up. In earlier periods, philosophers, physicians, moralists, and theologians commonly categorized feelings as 'passions' and 'affections'.

Pre-modern history tells how different philosophers believed in different ideologies. Buddhism believed that emotions occurred when an object is considered either attractive or repulsive. Stoic theories described them as irrational impulses coming from either good or bad. According to Aristotle, emotions corresponded to appetites or capacities. The Chinese believed that excessive emotions were harmful to vital organs. Avicenna studied the influence of emotions on health and behaviors in the 11th century.

Early modern views on emotion were developed in the 19th century and emotions were considered adaptive and were studied more frequently from an empiricist psychiatric perspective.

"*"I don't want to be at the mercy of my emotions. I want to use them, to enjoy them, and to dominate them."*
*— Oscar Wilde, The Picture of Dorian Gray*"

# III

# Those Feels

Emotions are a complex network. Especially they are least helpful when communicating. Even the wheels of emotions won't help you out on your first date. (Also please don't think about wheels of emotions on your first date). Reading or understanding facial expressions is a big deal. Have you ever wondered how two human bodies signal each other about their feelings?

While watching any movie, the actors work around emotions and get connected to their audience. Also, not everyone is a fan of the same genre. There exists a bridge between the liking and the emotion one tries to relate with it. The death of a superstar or any famous personality might affect differently to his fan following and the rest of the people. Winning any match or game has a momentary effect. The same follows for the lost game.

It might seem that emotions are the control box, not that we are in the anchor of the emotions completely all the time. We don't show emotions in every situation. They pop up and run away. Some are much more emotional than others, but even they have times when they are not feeling any emotion. Research says, at times emotions are so sudden that it exceeds the realization state. You might not notice that emotion or even react, for it is too slight.

So, why do those feel? If at some point there is no emotion, why do we even become emotional later? what triggers us to act like that?

Well, the only path for becoming emotional is when we sense something right or wrong or things that are going to affect our interest or well-being, that can be both worse or better, something that is going to happen.

*The vastness of the empty roads was eating her up. As Hunar walked briskly on the left side of the lane, she prayed for her safety. She didn't want to end up in any kind of problem after being already late for work. Like a hungry wolf searching for prey she widened her eyes and checked the road for vehicles now and then. Sadly, there wasn't a single soul roaming on the streets which devastated her. Soon the road turned into a ghastly area with a slimy black liquid spilling on its one side; the sight of dumped garbage made it even worst. She started shivering as if she was under a high fever. Suddenly, she saw a black stray dog coming towards her. Being an animal-phobic person all she could imagine was being bitten by the dog. She walked slowly with her head held high to reflect her righteousness. Surprisingly, the wild dog didn't bark! Then, she noticed the leather collar on his neck, he was domesticated. He had lost his owner. He started walking beside her like an old friend. She gathered the courage to look at his face. The jet-black dog was scared and was searching for a company in the deserted area. She caressed him gently and befriended him.*

The above incident is a great example of how emotions help us prepare for any circumstances without any second thoughts. If the girl had not monitored the situation, she might have ended up being attacked by the dog. Emotion thus acts as a superhero in all cases. Once the danger passed, you would still feel the fear churning away inside. It would take ten to fifteen seconds for those sensations to subside, and there would not be much you could do to cut that short. Like it took a few seconds for the girl to calm down and care for the dog.

How brain acts when you become emotional? During an incident that is bound to occur, emotions produce changes in parts of the brain, and then the whole body, right from facial expressions to voice, all are signaled by the brain. The changes in the autonomic nervous system, which regulates our heart rate, breathing, sweating, and many other bodily changes, prepares us for different actions.

All these changes are very abrupt and strong, as in the above example. Once the episode of emotion is over, it won't be as accurate as the first time. It will be impossible for you to understand what the brain did and how did it recognize the danger. You would only remember the actions you took. While describing the incident to someone, you would tell the concluding part and not how your facial expression changed or any other body sensations you had.

Emotions begin without our awareness of what is the process involved. But this boon can turn against us. If the process were slower, we might be aware of what was happening inside our brain; indeed, we might all know the answers to the questions related to emotions. But we wouldn't survive near-miss car accidents; we wouldn't be able to act quickly enough.

Emotion, a superhero continuously scans the surroundings around us and detects the wrong and right for our survival with extraordinary speed.

Expressing emotion and judging them have two different notions. Though facial expressions help a lot in decoding them these are not useful in every situation. The algorithm of understanding facial expression and emotions is resolved by Paul Ekman.

Paul Ekman, a psychologist and leading researcher on emotions, has explored the evolutionary and behavioral essences of anger, sadness, fear, surprise, disgust, contempt, and happiness. Dalai Lama with his notion of inner peace worked out with Paul Ekman to build an Atlas of Emotions that helps people to navigate through their emotions and attain a healthy mind.

Dr. Ekman after his thorough research and findings concluded that there were five broad categories of emotions — anger, fear, disgust, sadness, and enjoyment — and that each had an elaborate subset of emotional states, triggers, actions, and moods. These emotions were then visualized by cartography. Check out the website with the name atlas of emotions and check out your emotional awareness.

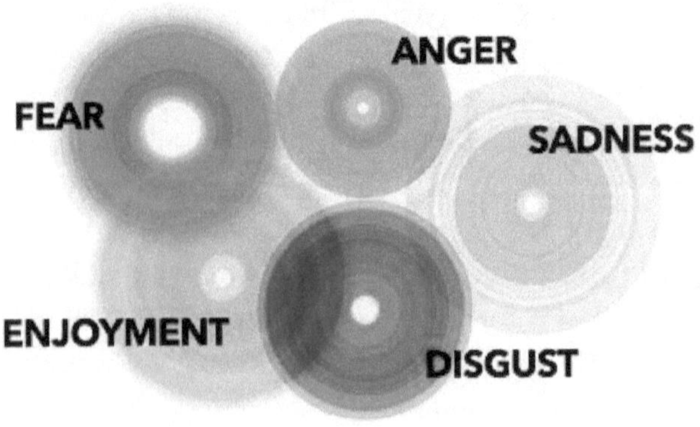


Atlas of Emotions

In 1976, Ekman also developed a test of emotion recognition called the Pictures of Facial Affect (POFA). In this test, he asked 110 Caucasian actors to portray the six universal emotions plus neutral expressions using black and white pictures. Earlier this test was used by him for cross-cultural research. Now, this test is used to study emotion recognition rates in normal and psychiatric populations around the world. Ekman eventually released a more culturally diverse set of stimuli called the Japanese and Caucasian Facial Expressions of Emotion (JACFEE).

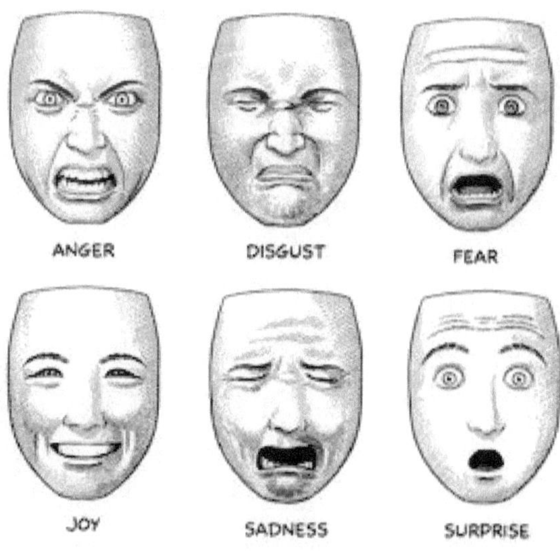


Six Basic Expressions

There are different views when it comes to animals as emotional beings. Historians believed - and many people still believe that there is a huge difference when considering the emotions of animals. Many think of it as a behavioral phenomenon. So, instead of assigning them as human emotions, it is better to be understood as stimulus-response theory.

Recent advances show a lot of improvement in animal-emotion research. The findings tell that animals do experience at least some degree of emotion. Technologies have helped observe different emotions exhibited by animals in their natural habitat. Their reaction to any triggering event is supposed to be an emotional one. Many agree these responses are not just instinctual in nature.

In other words, animals that rely on a group for survival must be more sensitive to what those around them are feeling, whether they're human or non-humans.

*"The world is a tragedy to those who feel, but a comedy to those who think."*
— **Horace Walpole**

# IV

# Journey of Emo-volution

Apart from being a naturalist, Charles Darwin turned out to be an early experimental psychologist.

Darwin believed the journey of emotions to be evolutionary in the history of mankind. He argued that all humans and non-human beings exhibit emotions through similar behaviors in his book *The Expression of the Emotions in Man and Animals*, published in 1872. As stated earlier, many psychologists, even today, agree with the Darwinian view on emotions.

This book corresponded with a French physician Guillaume-Benjamin-Amand Duchenne, who believed that human faces expressed at least 60 discrete emotions, each of which depended on its own dedicated group of facial muscles. In contrast, Darwin thought the facial muscles worked together to create a core set of just a few emotions.

To support his theory of evolution, Darwin studied the expression of emotions. He strongly believed that much like other traits, emotions also were evolved and adapted over a course of time. He worked on facial expressions by humans as well as animals after any event, and he also tried to establish a parallel relationship between these two.

As humans evolved, so did emotions. Different emotions evolved at different times. The two types of emotions namely primary and secondary emotions were discovered. Primary emotions are the body's first response and are usually very easy to identify because they are so strong, that include fear, happiness, sadness, and anger. Fear, which is a primal emotion, is associated with ancient parts of the brain and presumably evolved among our ancestors. Secondary emotions are a complex version of primary emotions. Like, relief comes after feeling joy or pride. A mother's love for her offspring often known as filial emotions evolved early in mammals. Some primates were evolved with social emotions, such as guilt and pride.

Emotion is expressing yourself, so are our habits. Darwin proposed three principles to understand this. Contract your eyebrow. Did you realize it changed your expression? Can you describe the emotion? Contracting eyebrow is a serviceable habit that helps to increase the field of vision or to prevent too much light from entering the eyes. This principle is the principle of serviceable habits.

Some habits we have are literally of no use. Like shrugging of shoulders. It signifies passive expression. This principle is the antithesis principle. Darwin proposed that some actions or habits are carried out merely because they are opposite in nature to a serviceable habit, but are not serviceable themselves.

The last is expressive habits. Some habits result in some sort of build-up in the nervous system. This build-up leads to the discharge of the excitement. Like tapping of finger and foot due to nervousness or vocal expressions or even anger. We do not always react to pain; some can endure a lot of pain without expressing or reacting to it.

Emotions developed through evolutionary processes and this has made it much easier for everyone to sit with them, appreciate them, and eventually to let them go.

*"Delight itself, however, is a weak term to express the feelings of a naturalist." — **Charles Darwin***

# V
# Emotional Ideologies

Scientists have had different opinions over emotions and their relation to expression.

Some believe that emotions and facial expressions go along, while some think it is all due to the mastermind brain. Let's find out.

The major theories of emotion can be grouped into three main categories: physiological, neurological, and cognitive.

- Physiological theories suggest that responses within the body are responsible for emotions.
- Neurological theories propose that activity within the brain leads to emotional responses.
- Cognitive theories argue that thoughts and other mental activities play an essential role in forming emotions

Then, we have different evolutionary theories, all work after Charles Darwin.

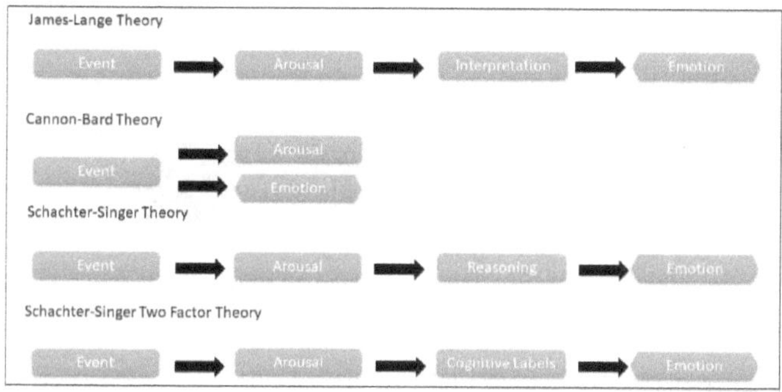


Theories of Emotion

# 1. *James-Lange Theory*

William James and Carl Lange, two American psychologists combined their theories. Both put forward that emotions are the results of physiological reactions to external events. They suggested that for humans to feel emotions, there have to be some physiological changes. Once these changes are determined, accordingly emotions are felt. Technically, they proposed that it was emotional stimuli that generate the feeling of emotion and not the other way round (remember, the complete opposite of Darwin's theory.)

Here's a James Lange Theory example:

You are walking down the alley and see an angry dog running towards you. Your heartbeat increases. So, according to this theory, you will conclude that you are scared because of your increased heart rate.

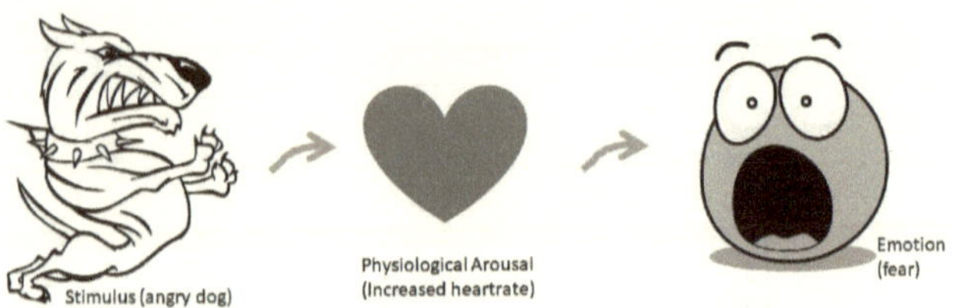


James-Lange Theory of Emotions

Consider this example. A couple decided to watch a movie together and due to some circumstances, the husband completely forgot about the date. He returns home only to find a 'frowned' wife sitting on a couch. He suddenly remembered the date and calms down his 'angry' wife. In this case, the man concluded that his wife is 'angry' due to her 'frowned' look.

Did you know physiological responses continue in an aroused state and take a longer time to settle back to normal levels in women as compared to men? That's why we generally state (and widely believe) that women are more emotional than men.

Not all scientists believed in this theory. Let's check out what critics has to say.

## 2. Cannon-Bard Theory

Walter Cannon was one of the scientists who proposed criticism against James-Lange theory, in the 1900s. He emphasized the role of the brain when reacting to certain events. He with his student, Philip Bard continued research on this and created a theory together. He suggested that it was possible to experience emotion even if the brain does not signal any bodily part. Completely relying on bodily responses was not the only way to express emotion. Two different emotions can be expressed by the same bodily reaction.

According to Cannon-Bard theory, humans recognize emotions and simultaneously undergo physiological responses such as perspiring, trembling, and tensing of muscles.

Remember thalamus (a small part of our brain) sends a message to the brain in response to a stimulus, resulting in a physiological reaction. Thalamus sends a reaction to the amygdala, which is responsible for processing strong emotions such as fear, pleasure, or anger. It might also send signals to the cerebral cortex, which controls conscious thought. Signals sent from the thalamus to the autonomic nervous system and skeletal muscles control physical reactions. These include sweating, shaking, or tense muscles. Sometimes, the Cannon-Bard theory is referred to as the thalamic theory of emotion.

In the previous angry dog example, there is a slight modification.

You are walking down the alley and see an angry dog running towards you. Your heartbeat increases and you immediately start running.

Cannon-Bard Theory of Emotion

Cannon and Bard simulated that bodily responses have no influence on emotion, but other studies showed otherwise. They also performed their studies on animals, and thus their theory could not be relied on. Moreover, the theory over-estimated the function of the thalamus in emotional processes, as there are other parts of the brain that are involved in emotions.

## 3. Schacter-Singer Theory

Stanley Schachter and Jerome Singer tested whether the same type of physiological activation (like adrenaline shot) could have different effects on people depending on the situational context.

Imagine yourself at a party. You are dancing happily with your friends. And suddenly someone insults you without any reason. The happy face will suddenly turn to an angry face, though the surrounding is a happy one.

According to the Schachter-Singer theory, emotions are a result of two factors:

- Physical processes in the body. These changes can include things like having your heart start beating faster, sweating, or trembling.
- A cognitive process, in which people try to interpret this physiological response by looking at their surrounding environment to see what could be causing them to feel this way. Like you might start looking here and there if there is a sudden increase in your heartbeat.

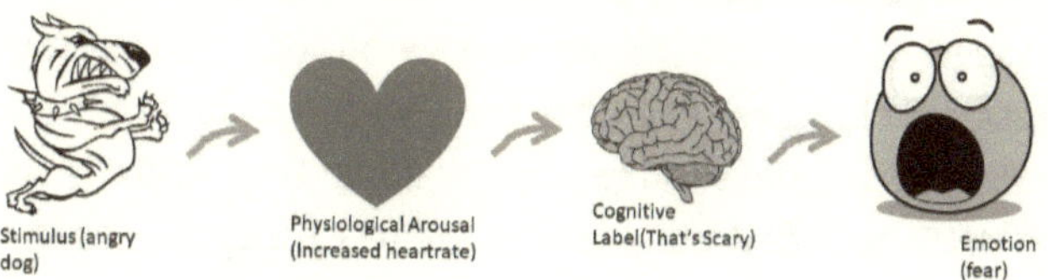


Schacter-Singer Theory of Emotion

Again looking at the angry dog example.

You are walking down the alley and see an angry dog running towards you. There is an increase in heartbeat. The brain then analyses that this situation is frightening and thus the emotion, i.e., you are afraid.

According to this theory, we usually take a clue from our surroundings to check out the situation and react likewise. Since these two scientists consider the environment as a second factor of detecting emotions, this theory is also called the two-factor theory of emotion. Although there is evidence that physiological activation can affect how we experience emotions, the available research has rather mixed results and leaves some questions unanswered.

## 4. *Facial Expression Theory*

How are you feeling until now, I mean reading this book? Bored? I wish you all could see the apologetic expression on my face.

Facial Expression theory explains how facial expressions are a way of communicating. Psychologists believe that there is a universal set of facial expressions which are formed vis face muscles and body muscles. The complex interaction between the brain and the nervous system produces different facial expressions. This is what Ekman suggested (*see chapter 3*). In 1978, Ekman and Friesen developed a method to identify emotions using facial expression changes. The observers were made to look for changes in people's micro-expressions that usually last from 1/15 to 1/25 of a second. According to Ekman, microexpression conveys true emotions. But these can turn into macro expressions within a fraction of seconds hiding the true nature of emotion.

Try to identify seven basic emotions from the faces below.

"*"Unexpressed emotions will never die. They are buried alive and will come forth later in uglier ways.*"
— **Sigmund Freud**"

# VI

# Wear That Mask

We all wear the mask of emotion. Let me explain what I am trying to say exactly. When was the last time you faked thank you on your birthday or anniversary to your a long distant relative? or when was the last time you made your friend feel like the Vogue model while trying a new dress? We all try to manage our emotions through multiple facial expressions. We usually think of the other person's feelings and intensify them while managing our own.

This is called masking your emotions. It means, emotion when communicating is totally different from the emotion that you are actually feeling. It has helped you all in a lot of situations, surely. For example, someone really close to your heart, demised and all you want to do is be all gloomy and stay at home. However, there is a job interview which you really can't miss, so you put on a happy and confident face and attend that interview. But deep down you will be completely miserable.

In many cases, you don't want to display your emotions at all (*thinking of a poker game*). You try to hide all possible emotions even if you are holding the highest rank card.

Such individuals display fewer emotions than they are actually feeling. Another great type of masking is simulation. I am sure this must have happened with everyone at least once. Your family decides to throw you a surprise graduation party and you happen to know everything about it. So, to avoid upsetting them you decide to go with the flow and act completely surprised.

*Humans! Falsifying whatever comes their way!*

Imagine your boss tripping on a wet floor. Though this is a very pretty funny situation, you and all your subordinates subdue your laughter. This is a typical example of an emotional display rule. There are cultural rules and etiquette for how, when, and where to express, or not express, certain emotions. Failing to follow emotional rules can lead others to possibly judge or be concerned for you. Like in the previous example, if you had laughed over your boss tripping, that might have led to losing your job. Other examples of this rule are, controlling your yawn in a lecture or telling your doctor about the weirdest symptom and the doctor trying to constraint his laughter.

In terms of gender differences, emotional rules may not be that justified. For example, men are "allowed" to yell, but women are judged for doing so. Women can cry, but men are often perceived as weak if they do so. *Sad reality!*

## Multiple Emotions

Emotions are not peerless, they always come in pairs or groups. One of your loose-lipped colleagues had the audacity to insult your group project. You will feel ashamed and anger will follow it. Such type of multiple emotions are necessary and happen most of the time. Emotions arise depending upon skills, aptitude, and abilities. So, it's natural they might come in groups. The language is to blame. There are almost no words to describe a cluster of emotions with different emotions. 'Tears of Joy'- this expression tells that a person is both happy and sad, but there is almost no such word to describe it. Though there is *nostalgia*- feeling sad over something happier that happened in the past.

## *Second-hand Emotions*

Let's praise other emotions. Happiness is considered as the only hero in the world of emotions and the rest of the emotions, especially anger as second emotion. If emotions were a school, then anger would be the guy who is always punished. In fact in the world of emotion, other than happiness all emotions are punishment guys. (*'Stay happy' nonsense!*)

Openly displaying anger might not always help you but yes it has got other purposes. The same is with fear, sadness, and other emotions. This happens usually, you get cranky suddenly, after crying after some annoying scene. So, in this situation anger acts as a protective emotion, and not second-hand emotion, which is very necessary! Anger jumps out in front of the real emotion 'sadness'. If someone jumps out to scare you, you just get scared for a moment and then smile or laugh back. Here happiness comes out for fear. This doesn't make happiness a second emotion. Similar is the case with all other emotions. They all have their own purpose.

When an action for a specific emotion is complete, new and different emotions will come to light, with different intensities obviously. Some may be in the form of a gift or skill or maybe as mood, or some as a call to immediate action. And thus, there will be more than one emotion active at any given time. Listed below are how emotions help us out in different situations.

| Emotional Skills | How do they help us? |
| --- | --- |
| Anger | Helps in setting boundaries, protect and restore what is important |
| Guilt and shame | Restores integrity, monitors behavior and make changes |
| Apathy | Covers anger when not able to set boundaries |
| Hatred | Tolerance level in self |
| Fear | Changes in the environment |
| Anxiety and worry | Pre-planning |
| Confusion | Let's one know when too much is going on |
| Jealousy | Choose and maintain relationships |
| Envy | Gain and maintain access to resources |
| Panic and terror | Protects one's life |
| Sadness | Let go of things that are not working, makes space for future work |
| Grief | Time needed to overcome losses |
| Situational Depression | Helps in slowing down and look out for whay things are not working |
| Happiness | Helps in moving forward |
| Contentment | Reminder that things are going well |
| Joy | Experience bliss with oneself and other. |

## *The Two Emotion Telltale*

Have you been ever divided into two emotions? Like feeling sad and happy at the same time. There is a high possibility of some of you being in a love-hate relationship. There are times when you feel like doing something and also completely avoid it.

Yes, procrastination!

Procrastination mostly recites mixed emotions. You may be dying to start a project, while at the same time harboring fears about not being able to complete it successfully. And this will make you stop. Something deep inside you forces you to a screeching halt. You still willingly take all the risks due to the thinkable results and benefits. However, yin and yan is the evildoer. The positives are made up by strong need from rejection or failure.

Confusion creates two or more emotions. While deciding over something you will be caught between such emotions that will be felt at the same time. Though one of the feelings will dominate the other.

*"Ek tarfa pyar ki taqat hi kuch aur hoti hai ... auron ke rishton ki tarah yeh do logon mein nahi bat'ti ... Sirf mera haq hai ispe"* - Ae Dil Hai Mushkil, 2016

(The power of one-sided love is something else... like other's relationship it doesn't matter between two people... only my right is there).

How many emotions can you identify from this dialogue from a Bollywood movie? The emotion of falling in love, or being in love, has to be seen as one of the most positive emotional states of all. Yet, if this emotion is not equivalent from the opposite side, can give rise to equally powerful negative emotion. Surely, movies will explain this in a better way.

Other instances can be, death of a person's alcoholic-abusive father. Though he might have not given you the best childhood, deep down you feel light-weighted for your manipulative father is out of your life now.

To conclude, we can feel two different emotions at the same time, though the intensity might differ from situation to situation. Even saying " you are so emotional" to anyone is technically incorrect. It can mean that you're angry, anxious, sad, fearful, or that your emotions change a lot. Due to lack of emotional vocabulary, saying you are emotional is very common.

*"Every day we have plenty of opportunities to get angry, stressed or offended. But what you're doing when you indulge these negative emotions is giving*

*something outside yourself power over your happiness. You can choose to not let little things upset you.*

**-Joel Osteen**"

# VII
# Emotional Drive

Human life is full of activities. Eating, drinking, working, only to name a few. But have you ever wondered what makes us behave as we do? What drives us to eat? What drives us toward sex? Is there a biological basis to explain the feelings we experience? Have you wondered as to- 'why do we need to go to work every day?' ' why do you like to party?' 'why does your mother stay up the whole night and care for you when you are feeling unwell? There is a purpose behind all these questions. All these activities are purposeful. These needs and wants are a path to achieve goals. A motive to drive towards our goal.

*Motivation- the driving force behind the energy required to complete a task.*

To achieve a level of particular contentment, psychologist Abraham Maslow suggested a hierarchy that each person must endeavor. As shown in the figure below, the lowest level needs must be fulfilled first. Once these are faced, safety is the priority followed by a sense of belonging and affection towards friends and family. After achieving these needs, one feels the urge to have self-esteem, confidence, and a feeling of self-worth. This is followed by the desire for knowledge and understanding and then order and beauty. The person finally moves towards self-actualization making him self-aware is socially responsive, and is open to the challenges of life.

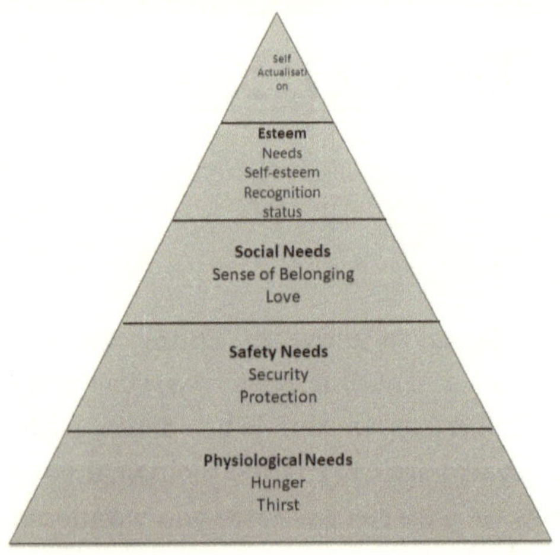


Maslow's hierarchy of needs

Like emotion, motivation is another tool of survival. Let's see the relationship between them.

Parents' love and affection towards their children motivates them to care. Sadness prevails after the death of a loved one whereas we experience anger at being treated unfairly. Emotions play an important role in our lives by motivating us and also indicate the reason for motivation. Thus, emotions and motivation go side by side. Both push us towards activity. Any situation that brings about a strong emotion is likely to motivate you to either repeat it or to avoid it.

Hunger, thirst, sleep- primary needs, and secondary needs like achievement, power, or approval are accompanied by satisfaction, joy, and pride- emotional reactions.

This is how motivation and emotion work conjointly.

- They move, activate, and help control and plan human behavior
- Emotion helps us to differentiate the needs and wants and things to avoid
- Emotion can serve as a motive. A crying child will soon get attention from his loved ones. Crying motivates the child to seek comfort
- Basic emotions and their expressions are universal in nature yet culture provide guidelines towards how and when to show emotions

Both emotions and motivation originate from the same Latin root, meaning 'to move. Both are associated with arousal and bodily responses that are created by the autonomic nervous system. Considering the fact that emotions and motivation involve arousal, they drive our behavior.

Biological motivations are the motivation for food, water, and sex. Another type of motivation influences behavior like social approval, achievement, taking or avoiding risks. We follow them because they are rewarding. And motivation does make us feel good. They act as a series of behavioral responses that lead us to attempt to reduce drives and to attain goals by comparing our current state with the desired end state. Consider an airconditioner, the way it regulates room temperature, the human body tries to maintain equilibrium with goals, arousal, and drives. When a goal is to awaken, our behavior automatically turns in a way that attempts to meet the goal. Like, in case you are hungry, you start seeking food. Once the goal is achieved, the corresponding behavior stops.

Personal and social motivations are also looked upon as goals or drives. For example, skipping a day to study for an exam, working harder to achieve the relevant goal. When feeling lonely, suddenly we are motivated to be around people and try to socialize. In most of the cases, our emotions and motivations operate out of our conscious awareness to guide our behaviour.

*"Rock bottom became the solid foundation in which I rebuilt my life.*

*—J.K. Rowling"*

# VIII

# The Roller Coaster Ride

Emotions dance. Yes for everyone. At times, in some situations, you may feel happy, and then sad. This happens with everyone and there is no shame in accepting the fact that "*I am not in the mood, right now.*"

A sudden change in an emotional state is mood swings. The emotions like to go under a roller coaster ride. This is not their fault. There are many reasons for people to go up and down this road. Not only women, but men are also prone to mood swings. Reasons? A lot.

- Lifestyle changes
- Experiencing a relevant life change, job change, or moving out to a different place
- Stress
- Less sleep
- Eating less healthy
- Medications impacting mood and sleep

If mood swings persist for a long time, then it can indicate an elementary condition. These affect irrespective of gender, though some may be severe in females. In their mind people have categorized mood swings as harmless and take them very lightly, however, they can be intense as well. These swings if not looked upon, can turn into disorders. Not to be treated as something endemic, mood swing is a normal mental condition. It is the continued progress of a person's mood. When these fluctuations occur at an extreme level, they start interfering with the regular functioning of the body. At such an instance, these symptoms should not be ignored and must be discussed with counselors, once the reason is known.

Current lifestyle has led to an unhealthy diet and improper cycle. These then have a strong impact on physical and mental health. Lack of sleep leads to fatigue for a long period. Such an individual would then experience low motivation and a high level of anxiety for a considerable amount of time. The energy of such a person is not restored until a good sound sleep.

Now, do you get why new moms look frustrated all the time? NO SLEEP!

There are many facts one must know about mood swings.

1. They are not mood disorders. They are not always severe, sometimes a little attention is enough rather than a serious treatment. It is a very short-lived non-medical condition. However, mood disorders need medical practitioners.

2. Low Vitamin D and calcium can trigger mood swings. Calcium helps in maintaining mood and its deficiency can cause irritation and tension in humans.

3. Odd working hours make people more prone to mood swings and irritation. Anxiety is the culprit here.

The interpretation of whether a person is suffering from mood swings or disorders depends upon the intensity and frequency of mood variations. Physical and mental health examinations can rule all out possibilities. Physical health problems such as hormonal imbalance, diabetes, PCOD, etc., may cause fatigue conditions and extreme mood swings. This is a serious thing, a mood disorder! The majority of the population doesn't consider this as serious health trouble.

What can you do from your side?

Shift towards a healthier lifestyle. It is difficult but not impossible.

1. Regular Exercise: This is a necessity. 4-5 days every week is sufficient. Absolutely anything that works out for you. Gym, cycling, yoga, jogging, swimming, meditation, etc. Endorphins (feel-good hormones) uplifts the mood.

2. Balanced Diet: Well-balanced diets avoid an abrupt increase or decrease in blood glucose level which helps in maintaining mood stability. 5-6 smaller meals are the key.

This boosts metabolism and helps in controlling blood sugar. As said earlier, increase intake of calcium has been proven to ease emotional fluctuations related to pre-menstrual syndrome.

3. Proper Sleep Cycle: Beauty sleep! A sound sleep is required for energy restoration as well as mental healing of a person. Lack of sleep is capable of making a person lethargic and irritable whereas proper sleep keeps a person energized and motivated throughout the day.

4. Track Mood Swing Trigger: You can always maintain a diary or journal to track your mood daily. This is fun. For people with zero artistic skills, people have developed apps to track mood. Try this for a week at least, you will get to see how moody you are actually. It feels good to see when the app tells you how many times you have been happy, sad, angry, etc in a week or month or even a year.

5. Therapy: I hope this be the last step for everyone. Psychotherapists build a relationship with the sufferer and channelize the thought process of the sufferer in a positive direction. In the therapy sessions, sufferers undergo multiple counseling sessions, which help in dealing with the problem of mood swings.

Mood swings in men are becoming more common now. Men who are dealing with alcoholism or a different substance abuse disorder often experience mood changes. The male body reacts in a way similar to a woman's body in response to hormonal fluctuations – primarily in response to shifts in the male sex hormone, testosterone. Men do appear to go through a similar stage in life where testosterone levels plummet. This phase has been called *andropause*.

Though there is no clear point that defines andropause. Slowly over the time, the male body slows testosterone production, but it doesn't stop completely. This may lead to an extended period where men experience symptoms, including chronic or even sudden and drastic changes in mood.

Swings are good and are a part of life. Some degree of variation in mood is normal. But changes in mood shouldn't interfere with the quality of life.

> ""Emotions come and go and can't be controlled so there's no reason to worry about them. That in the end, people should be judged by their actions since, in the end, it was actions that defined everyone."
> — **Nicholas Sparks**"

# IX

# Soudness of mind

Let's talk about mental health. World Mental Health Day is celebrated on October, 10. Mental Health was brought into the limelight by two French Scientists in 1908. Mental health includes our emotional, psychological, and social well-being. It affects how we think, feel, and act. It also help determine how we handle stress, relate to others, and make choices.

This is how a mentally ill person might look like.

- Eating or sleeping too much or too little
- Pulling away from people and usual activities
- Having low or no energy
- Feeling numb or like nothing matters
- Having unexplained aches and pains
- Feeling helpless or hopeless
- Smoking, drinking or using drugs more than usual
- Feeling unusually confused, forgetful, on edge, angry, upset, worried, or scared
- Yelling or fighting with family and friends

- Experiencing severe mood swings that cause problems in relationships
- Having persistent thoughts and memories you can't get out of your head
- Hearing voices or believing things that are not true
- Thinking of harming yourself or others
- Inability to perform daily tasks like taking care of your kids or getting to work or school

Emotions affect our mental health. Negative emotions such as unexpressed thoughts or a feeling of hopelessness affect our mental health. There are many myths about mental health. Let's clear out those first.

## 1. Myth: Children don't experience mental health problems

Fact: Very young children have shown early warning signs of mental health. Though they are diagnosable and are usually the product of biological, psychological, or social factors. Before a child turns 14, half of the mental health disorders can be observed, and about three-fourth before age 24.

## 2. Myth: People with mental health problems are violent and unpredictable.

Fact: Most people with mental illness are not violent, and only 3-5% of violent acts can be linked to a serious mental illness. People with severe mental illness are over 10 times more likely to be victims of violent crime than the general population. You probably know someone with a mental health problem and don't even realize it, because many people with mental health problems are highly active and productive people in the community.

*3. Myth: People with mental health needs, even those who are managing their mental illness, cannot tolerate the stress of holding down a job.*

Fact: They are as productive as other employees.

*4. Myth: Personality weakness or character flaws cause mental health problems. People with mental health problems can snap out of it if they try hard enough.*

Fact: Many factors contribute to mental health problems, including:

- Biological factors, such as genes, physical illness, injury, or brain chemistry
- Life experiences, such as trauma or a history of abuse
- Family history of mental health problem

*5. Myth: There is no hope for people with mental health problems. Once a friend or family member develops mental health problems, he or she will never recover.*

Fact: People with mental health problems can get better and many recover completely. There are more treatments, services, and community support systems than ever before, and they work.

*6. Myth: Therapy and self-help are a waste of time. Why bother when you can just take a pill?*

Fact:Treatment for mental health problems varies depending on the individual and could include medication, therapy, or both.

*7. Myth: I can't do anything for a person with a mental health problem.*

Fact: You can help them by

- Reaching out and letting them know that you are available to help
- Learning and sharing facts about mental health, especially if you hear something that isn't true
- Treating them with respect, just as you would anyone else
- Refusing to define them by their diagnosis or using labels such as "crazy"

*8. Myth: Prevention doesn't work. It is impossible to prevent mental illnesses.*

Fact: Promoting the social-emotional well-being of children and youth leads to:

- Higher overall productivity
- Better educational outcomes
- Lower crime rates
- Stronger economies
- Lower health care costs

- Improved quality of life
- Increased lifespan
- Improved family life

## *What Is Emotional Health?*

Emotional health is having both an awareness of your emotions and the ability to manage and express those feelings in an age-appropriate manner. This health cannot be fixed instantly, it requires a lot of steps for its improvement. For example, you can try to identify the positives in situations that are not as per your wish or work on developing your strengths instead of focusing on any perceived weaknesses.

Both mental and emotional health may sound the same to our ears but they are very different.

1: Processing Information Versus Expressing Emotion

Mental health: the ability of the mind to process and understand information and experiences

Emotional health: the ability to manage and express the emotions that arise from what you have learned and experienced.

2: One Can Thrive While the Other Struggles

You can experience mental health issues while maintaining good emotional health, and vice versa. For example, you could struggle with daily tasks due to lack of energy (mental health) but you still try to find effective ways to manage that lack of energy (emotional health).

3: The Scope of the Two Terms

Mental health is the ability to carefully reason through decisions and maintain a steady, focused attention span while emotional health is a more focused definition of actively understanding and managing your emotions.

Our thoughts and actions expose our emotions. The feelings that turn us inside out or the other way round are determined by internal thinking. There is a trigger that that gets pulled out. It can be people places or things. Harboring the right emotions is thus key to maintaining harmony in your mental and physical environment.

All the reactions we exhibit are the response to the way we think, feel, and act. This is one of its kind of mind/body connections. When you are stressed, anxious, or upset, your body reacts in a way that might tell you that something isn't right. Such stressful situations can release a surge of hormones in your body. We have already seen how everything is controlled by a tiny part of our brain known as the hypothalamus that reacts to any stimuli. It reacts to the stressor by sending out signals that trigger the production of stress hormones. If this is chronic, stress can take a toll on your body and can elevate the levels of the stress hormone and can lead to stroke, heart attack, and depression.

Negative emotions can give a tough time to your heart and double the chances of heart disease. Rather than being a goal, emotional health is more of a process. No, it is not about always being in a good mood. It is all about how to deal with the good, the bad, and everything in between. Negative emotions can only be dealt with by accepting them and embracing the negative states. Along with this, one should engage with the activities that can double-take these not-so-wanted emotions.

Expressing and speaking up with family members. Opt for journaling(my favorite). And there is always a mood tracker app. Positive emotions are like flowers, you can cultivate them, play with them the way you want to.

"*"Sometimes the people around you won't understand your journey. They don't need to, it's not for them.*"

**– Joubert Botha**"

# END NOTE

Do you remember your facial expression or emotion while lying?

Ohh, yes everyone lies.

Facts? Approximately 4% of people are complete liars and they could do it well. Do you want to know how to find a cheater or a liar? Follow the next letters.

Let's say you're chatting with your colleague's significant other. She boastfully mentions that she was invited to one of the celebrities' weddings. You ask how the big chocolate cake tasted, when, in fact, you know it was a white vanilla cake decorated with flowers. If the person said he loved the chocolate, you've got a liar in front of you.

This is a technique called 'volatile conundrum'. It is a subtle technique to bring out a liar or how truthful the person is. So, the technique lies in asking questions to which you already know the answer. It should be a false statement so that, if the person agrees with you, you know they're lying, and if the person disagrees, you can verify that they're truthful.

Using this technique several times might land you up in trouble, though. You can use it every once in a while when you sense something's out of place during a talk with someone. Be very normal! Like there should be no hint of letting the person know about your secret of enjoying the preceding conversation.

In the above example, if the other person was, in fact, telling the truth, and in case you were wrong about your suspicions. You don't need to worry, volatile conundrum has an escape clause.

Suppose the person doesn't remember the chocolate cake from the wedding but was totally describing the art and taste of some other flavored cake. Your doubts would be cleared and you would realize that the person actually went to the wedding. Also, you got to get out of the situation by saying that you thought it was chocolate cake.

Try this next time, you feel someone is lying.

$$\wr\wr$$

Are you emotionally intelligent? How do you develop emotional intelligence?

Some people have the ability to understand and influence emotions. People with such traits can do the same with others too. It has basic five components - self-awareness, self-regulation, empathy, motivation, and social skills. You can identify if the person or if you are emotional intelligent:

- Viewed as an empathetic person by others
- Excellent problem solver
- Not afraid to be vulnerable and share your feelings
- Set boundaries and aren't afraid to say "no"
- Can get along with people in different situations
- Able to shrug off a bad moment and move on
- Ask open-ended questions
- Can accept constructive criticism without making excuses or blaming others
- Outstanding listener
- Not afraid to admit your mistakes and apologize
- Self-motivated
- Understand your actions and behaviors

Listing five ways in which you can boost your emotional intelligence.

1. The Emotoscope Feeling Chart- a guide to the meaning of dozens of emotions. It breaks down the focus and purpose of dozens of emotions. Take, for example, feeling overwhelmed. I often over-commit and find myself feeling overwhelmed. It's easy to move around in that feeling and say, "I feel overwhelmed because of all these reasons: x, y and z." The beauty of the Emotoscope Feeling Chart is that it provides insight into what that emotion is telling me to do. In the case of feeling overwhelmed, it's to prioritize. The Emotoscope Feeling Chart is the perfect resource to help you master that step and cultivate emotional intelligence.

2. Jot down each of your day's best things, worst things, and what you're looking forward to.

3. When faced with a dilemma or decision, generate at least 3 options to consider. This will increase your decision-making skills.

4. More Empathy, Less Sympathy. Empathy is recognizing and appropriately responding to others. Sympathetic responses are like– offering advice, reasons to look on the bright side, etc. Whereas an empathetic response often means just sitting there and being with that person, validating what they're feeling.

5. So another trick to growing emotional intelligence is to pretend like you're making a decision for a friend or observing your life. This technique is the Solomon Paradox.

Some people are blessed with this emotional intelligence, and for the rest, there is always a way to grow more.

There are over 3000 words for feelings in English. How many are you feeling now? And what is that feeling trying to tell you? I sincerely hope, there would be at least one of the emotions you must be feeling after reading this small paperback.

How expressive emotions are! It is completely alright if you cannot express them, you are not alone in this universe.

Embrace those vibes. They are definitely trying to tell you something.

# REFERENCES

- Bertolote J. The roots of the concept of mental health. World Psychiatry. 2008;7(2):113-116. doi:10.1002/j.2051-5545.2008.tb00172.x
- Daniel L. (2011). Psychology Second Edition. New York: Worth Publishers. p. 310. ISBN 978-1429237192.
- Ekman, P. (1972). Universals and cultural differences in facial expressions of emotions. In Cole, J. (Ed.), *Nebraska Symposium on Motivation* (pp. 207-282). Lincoln, NB: University of Nebraska Press.
- Ekman, P. & Friesen, W. V. (1971). Constants across cultures in the face and emotion. *Journal of Personality and Social Psychology, 17(2),* 124-129.
- Ekman, P., Friesen, W. V., & Tomkins, S. S. (1971). Facial affect scoring technique: first validity study. . *Semiotica, 3,* 37-58.
- Ekman, P. (1970).Universal facial expressions of emotions. *California Mental Health Research Digest, 8(4),* 151-15
- M. Clynes et al. (eds.), Emotions and Psychopathology, Springer Science+Business Media New York 1988
- Papez, J. W. (1995). "A proposed mechanism of emotion. 1937 [classical article]". The Journal of Neuropsychiatry and Clinical Neurosciences. 7 (1): 103–12
- Plutchik, Robert (1980), Emotion: Theory, research, and experience: Vol. 1. Theories of emotion, 1, New York: Academic
- Schmidt LA (1999). "Frontal brain electrical activity in shyness and sociability". Psychological Science. 10 (4): 316–20

- Turner JH (2009). "The sociology of emotion: Basic Theoretical arguments". Emotion Review. 1 (4): 340–54